First Facts®

Staying Safe

Staying Safe on the School Bus

by Lucia Raatma

CAPSTONE PRESS
a capstone imprint

First Facts is published by Capstone Press,
1710 Roe Crest Drive, North Mankato, Minnesota 56003.
www.capstonepub.com

Library of Congress Cataloging-in-Publication Data
Raatma, Lucia.
  Staying safe on the school bus / by Lucia Raatma.
      p. cm. — (First facts. Staying safe)
  Includes bibliographical references and index.
  Summary: "Discusses rules and techniques for school bus safety"—Provided by publisher.
  ISBN 978-1-4296-6823-1 (library binding)
  ISBN 978-1-4296-7199-6 (paperback)
  1. School children—Transportation—Safety measures—Juvenile literature. 2. School buses—
Safety measures—Juvenile literature. I. Title.
  LB2864.R23 2012
  363.12'59—dc22   2011006046

Editorial Credits
Rebecca Glaser and Christine Peterson, editors; Ted Williams, designer;
    Svetlana Zhurkin, media researcher; Laura Manthe, production specialist

Photo Credits
Capstone Studio/Karon Dubke, cover, 6, 12–13, 14, 16–17; Dreamstime/Sonya Etchison, 10; Getty
Images/Gary Buss, 8; Shutterstock/Cheryl Casey, 4–5; klohka, 1; Maria Dryfhout, 18; Stephen
Mahar, 20; Wendy Kaveney Photography, 9

Essential content terms are **bold** and are defined at the bottom of the spread where
they first appear.

Printed in the United States of America in North Mankato, Minnesota.
022013   007194R

Table of Contents

Here Comes The Bus

They're big, yellow, and fun to ride. School buses are also a safe way to get to and from school. School buses pick kids up near their homes in the morning. When school is done, they bring them home again. Just follow a few rules, and you can stay safe on the school bus.

Know the Danger Zone

Stay safe around school buses by keeping out of the danger zone. The danger zone is any area near the school bus where the driver can't see you. Stay at least 10 steps away from the bus. Always cross the street in front of a bus. Look left, right, then left again before crossing.

At the Bus Stop

Children wait for school buses at bus stops. Bus stops can be street corners or driveways. Bus drivers know to stop at these places.

Get to the bus stop early. Walk to the bus stop with friends or a trusted adult. At the bus stop, wait in line quietly. Don't push others or run around.

trusted adult—a grown-up you know who is honest and reliable

All Aboard

Once the bus stops, stand still until the driver opens the doors. Stay in line, and wait for your turn to get on the bus. Make sure your backpack or clothes don't have long strings. These strings could get caught in the door. Hold the handrail as you step onto the bus. Find a seat quickly, and sit down.

handrail—a narrow rail that can be held for support

The School Bus Driver

The school bus driver keeps kids safe. To be safe, the driver needs to pay attention to the road. Always listen to the bus driver. Talk quietly, and don't bounce around. Loud noise or a lot of movement could distract the driver.

distract—to draw attention away from something

Stay Seated

When riding on a school bus, always stay seated. Keep your back against the seat, and face forward. Don't stick your arms or head out the window. Put your backpack and other items on or under your seat. Keep the aisle open.

aisle—a walkway between seats

Time For School

You're excited for school, but don't rush to get off the bus. Wait for the bus to stop. Then stand up. Wait patiently in line. Don't push or shove others.

CAP. 77
EW 15,7

Hold the handrail as you leave the bus. Take 10 steps to get into a safe place away from the bus.

The Trip Home

When school ends, it's time to get back on the bus. Follow the same safety rules on the ride home. Once you leave the bus, keep walking. Don't go back onto the bus, even if you forgot something. If you drop something, don't bend down to pick it up. First, get the driver's attention. Then ask for help.

Emergencies

School buses are safe, but emergencies can happen. Drivers know how to keep you safe. Listen to the driver, and stay calm. Go to the bus' **emergency exit**, if needed.

emergency exit—a door or window that can be used to get off a bus in case of a crash, fire, or other emergency

Hands On:
Bus Safety Poster

Share what you know about school bus safety by making a safety poster. You can hang the poster at home or school. The poster will remind others of the safety rules.

What You Need

markers
paper

What You Do

1. Choose one or two safety rules you would like to include on a poster.
2. With a marker, write the rule down on a piece of paper.
3. Draw a school bus, stop sign, or other pictures to illustrate the rule. Color your drawings with markers.
4. Ask a parent or teacher to hang the poster at home or school.
5. Make more posters to show other school bus safety rules.

Glossary

aisle (ILE)—a walkway between seats

distract (DIS-trakt)—to draw attention away from something

emergency exit (i-MUHR-juhn-see EG-zit)—a door or window that can be used to get off a bus in case of a crash, fire, or other emergency

handrail (HAND-rail)—a narrow rail that can be held for support

trusted adult (TRUHS-tud uh-DUHLT)—a grown-up you know who is honest and reliable

Read More

Johnson, Jinny. *Being Safe.* Now We Know About. New York: Crabtree Pub. Company, 2010.

Mattern, Joanne. *Staying Safe on the School Bus.* Safety First. Milwaukee: Weekly Reader Early Learning Library, 2007.

Rissman, Rebecca. *We Can Stay Safe.* Chicago: Heinemann Library, 2010.

Internet Sites

FactHound offers a safe, fun way to find Internet sites related to this book. All of the sites on FactHound have been researched by our staff.

Here's all you do:

Visit *www.facthound.com*

Type in this code: 9781429668231

 **Super-cool stuff!** Check out projects, games and lots more at
www.capstonekids.com

Index